C000137949

LAUGH?
I Nearly Went To Bradford!

by

Tom Clinton

BRADFORD LIBRARIES & INFORMATION SERVICE

Dedication

This book is dedicated to the community and the
spirit of Bradford that makes it a special place
in which to be.

© Tom Clinton 1991

ISBN 0 907733 27 7

About the Author

Tom Clinton, aged 49, was born in Liverpool. He joined the Royal Navy when he was 18 years old and later worked for BBC Television in London before moving to West Yorkshire. He currently works for Bradford Metropolitan Council. From 1986 - 1988 Tom was seconded from his Council duties to act as Campaign Director of the *Bradford's Bouncing Back!* Campaign.

Author's appreciation

For their many and different contributions towards the *Bradford's Bouncing Back!* campaign and for helping this book to become a reality I would like to express my appreciation to the following people:

Jane Whittaker, *Arts Marketing Officer, Bradford Arts, Museums and Libraries Division*
Donald Woodcock, *Chief Executive, Bradford Chamber of Commerce*
Terry Quinn, *ex-Editor, Telegraph & Argus*
Dennis Walsh, *Briggs & Hill Ltd.*
Gordon Moore, *ex-Chief Executive, Bradford Metropolitan District Council*
David Hockney, *Bradford-born artist*
Roger Suddards, *Bradford Solicitor*
Sir John Harvey-Jones MBE, *Chancellor, Bradford University*
David Jones, *Chief Executive, Next plc*
Mike Glover, *Editor, Telegraph & Argus*
Jean Hunter, *National Museum of Photography, Film & Television, Bradford*
Dr. Mike Kelly, *ex-Lord Provost, Glasgow*
Judith Donovan, *JDA Ltd*
John Piercy, *Littlewoods Stores Ltd*
David Walters
Peter Owthwaite
Sally Wolfe, *ex-Bradford Libraries*
Jim Greenhalf, *Telegraph & Argus*

Photographic credits

The photographs shown on pages 19, 22, 23, 29, 31, 35 and 40 are reproduced by kind permission of Bradford's *Telegraph & Argus*.

The photograph shown on page 28 is courtesy of David Hockney.

The photographs shown on pages 34 and 38 are courtesy of Tim Smith, Bradford Hertiage Recording Unit.

The photograph shown on page 41 is courtesy of the Alhambra Theatre, Bradford.

Foreword

The book is divided into parts instead of chapters. This is deliberate because the chronological sequence of the events I describe is of less importance than the fact that they actually occurred at all. So those looking for a straightforward historical account will, I'm afraid, be disappointed. I have sought to explain how such events impacted upon the image of Bradford. In doing this I refer to "image" and "self-esteem" because the two things are so closely linked and, in my view, damage to one means damage to the other. If I wished any lessons to be learnt from this book it would be that a community is ultimately responsible for the way others perceive it. It is far too easy in this over-communicated society for a city's image to become the "property" of others (e.g. the media). If a city's image is perceived as negative then it becomes easy meat for anyone who wishes to pour more scorn on it and so the bad image is perpetuated — unless the target fights back. That's what we did in Bradford and must continue to do. Bradford is not quite paradise yet.

Tom Clinton
Bradford
West Yorkshire
England

May 1991

Contents

Introduction 1

Part One — A Much Maligned City 3
Brave and Spirited People 3
The biggest village in the country 4
Riches to Rags 7

Part Two — Dark Days 9
The murderer Sutcliffe 9
The Honeyford Affair 10
A terrible fire 11

Part Three — No Ordinary Council Report 13

Part Four — Bouncing Back 15
"We need to change our image" 15
Tales from a campaign 27
Measuring the success 42

Part Five — Turning the Corner 45

Part Six — The Community Celebrates Itself 49

Epilogue 53

..... and another view 55

Introduction

Imagine. You're driving along a moorside road, seemingly in the middle of nowhere and surrounded by rough wild landscape. You are a stranger to this part of the country. Perhaps you are on a business trip or visiting friends who have recently moved to the District. Below you, to your left and in the valley bottom, a distant road curves alongside the river before it climbs the steep sloping crag on the other side of the valley. It seems to be heading for a cluster of buildings which looks like a remote farm. The little specks in the surrounding green fields turn out to be a mixture of sheep, cattle and horses.

It's been raining and what's left of the resultant mist is slowly rolling up the hillside to your right, its place taken by pale sunshine. You are aware that there are sheep grazing on the roadside and, without warning, one of them darts in front of your car. Your foot hits the brake and you swerve onto the grass bank missing a dry stone wall by inches. Just to make sure there has been no damage you stop and get out of your car. The grey woolly beast seems unharmed and has lumbered off to join its compatriots grazing further up the hillside. They all stop and stand staring at you. You feel as if you are invading their privacy, like some uninvited guest. There are no other cars on the road. No houses. No people. Just you and some nervous sheep.

There is a silence broken only by the occasional shrill, whistling call of a bird. You think it may be a curlew although you can't recall ever having heard one before. There is a chill in the wind and you fantasise slightly about being trapped on this hillside in a snow blizzard or a howling gale. Your attention is drawn towards a large official looking sign on the roadside a few yards ahead. The sheep scatter as you walk through the springy heather in order to read what the sign says. The sign, topped by a colourful heraldic coat of arms reads *City of Bradford Metropolitan Council - Baildon Moor.*

You are rather surprised.

It's not at all what you had expected of a place called Bradford.

Part One

A Much Maligned City

"Brave and spirited people"

The first day of April 1974 was not just April Fool's Day. It was also the day upon which Bradford Metropolitan District Council was born. This was the result of a new piece of government legislation which was designed to produce a more effective and economic way to manage local government services.

Towns and villages in this part of West Yorkshire, that had previously held Urban Council status, found themselves part of something called "Bradford". Some of them have been resentful ever since and refer scornfully to the date of birth of the "new baby". There were many things they didn't like about their new enforced marriage with the City of Bradford and much of this was to do with its image. There was no way that anyone from Keighley or Ilkley, for example, would admit to coming from BRADFORD. After all — they had their pride to think of.

Whilst many of them perhaps worked there or used its facilities, admitting that you actually CAME from Bradford was somehow difficult to admit to. I mean, the place was a scruffy dying town "clinging desperately to the side of the wind swept Pennines", wasn't it? Surely it was full of empty, crumbling mills and dirty cobbled streets? And wasn't the place full of "foreigners" who had come to steal all our jobs? Who on earth would want to live and work in a dump like Bradford?

Dervla Murphy, the journalist and traveller, wrote in the *You* magazine (Mail on Sunday) on 23rd November, 1986:

"My London friends reacted strongly when they heard I would be moving to a bedsitter in Manningham, Bradford to research a book on race relations. "You're mad" said one. "Why do you have to go UP THERE?" Another said "Oh well, your work will be interesting. I just hope you're SAFE!"

and

"Walking uphill I paused at intervals to look down at an expanding cityscape of ugly factories and mill chimneys . . . Then, turning a corner, it seemed for a moment that I was hallucinating. Directly ahead rose the improbable Italianate magnificence of Lister's Mill — surely England's loveliest monument to the Industrial Age."

Ms Murphy then refers to the city's social and economic plight and finishes her article by saying:

"Logically, therefore, I should have been depressed by my months UP THERE. But Bradford is a place of brave and spirited people who know that, given half a chance, they can make their city flourish again."

❖❖❖

There were many local stories, no doubt apocryphal, that demonstrated the way locals and visitors viewed Bradford. Like the one about the hotel in Eastbourne. (This was told to the writer by two different and independent sources). A well known bus tour operator ran a coach through several major cities, picking up tourists on the way south. The coach commenced its journey in Leeds, then on to Bradford and then proceeded south through Sheffield, Nottingham, Birmingham, Coventry and other major connurbations, picking up passengers on the way to the hotel in Eastbourne. The first night in the hotel saw a welcoming dinner for the guests in the ballroom. 'Mine host' took to the stage and, aided by a microphone, introduced the new arrivals. "I know we have people here from Birmingham (or Leeds, Nottingham etc). As each place was mentioned, there was a roll of drums and the respective guests cheered and made their jovial presence felt by their fellow guests.

The announcements went on "... and we are also very pleased to have with us a group of people from ... BRADFORD! The drums dutifully rolled. There was total silence from the Bradford group. They had no wish to be announced in this way because they KNEW what would happen next. And it did. There were cries from all over the ballroom ...

"Where's your passport?"

"Why haven't you got your turbans on, then?"

"Eeh bah gum, let's have some black pudding to celebrate."

"No! — all they eat is curry UP THERE."

"Get a bloody job!"

and so on and much worse. Cruel comments thinly disguised as humour. Racism both covert and otherwise. The holiday for the people from Bradford was already ruined.

Bradford — a laughing stock. Finished. Washed up. A place with no hope, no future. A place fit only to be scorned.

In the mid 70's that's how much the outside world viewed Bradford and its people. Perhaps Bradfordians could learn to live with the jokes. Put up with the jibes and the myths. But there was something worse than feeling ashamed about coming from Bradford and that was the danger that even Bradfordians would begin to believe the myths. Maybe Bradford really WAS on its knees and finished. Maybe the downward spiral of gloom and despair was irreversible.

Maybe.

"The biggest village in the country"

Bradford is one of those places whose existence and success depended so much on its physical and geographical location. Located in a basin at the junction of two dales (Airedale and Wharfedale) Bradford is surrounded by hills. To the west they reach a height of over 1,000 ft whilst eastwards the land levels out to around 600 ft.

The rocks upon which the city is built not only give Bradford an attractive rugged terrain but also include a rich deposit of coals and ironstones upon which the 19th century economic surge was dependent. Earlier than this, the geography of the land determined where neolithic tribes were to put down their markers and settlements. Examination of pre-Norman conquest field maps shows just how the modern day Bradford city map still respects those earlier geographical boundaries. Many of the major roads still take seemingly illogical twists and turns because of medieval pathways and hedges long since buried.

To this day the whole metropolitan district (370 sq km) contains quite separate towns, villages and hamlets all fiercely proud of their history and their place in the Bradford of today. Someone once described Bradford as being "the biggest village in the country" and perhaps its basin-like setting encourages this point of view.

❖❖❖

Early in the 16th century Bradford was already known as a place that depended much on textiles for its economic and social survival. However this was very much a cottage based "industry" and to the east of Bradford the focus was on the production of white and coloured cloth. Towards the west and the Pennines it was the production of worsted that predominated.

The weavers lived in stone built cottages often two or three storeys high, with tall windows in front of which their looms would be situated. In Daniel Defoe's *Tour of Great Britain* he describes the Bradford scene: "At every considerable house was a manufactory, or wash house … They also had a dyeing house, scouring shops … every clothier must necessarily keep a horse, perhaps two, to fetch home his wool and his provisions from the market and to carry his yarn from the spinners, his manufactures to the fulling mill, and when finished, to the market to be sold.

Each week the cloth maker would make a piece of cloth which was brought to market "being compelled to sell the same at the weekend and with the money received to provide stuff wherewith to make another the following week".

In 1773 there was sufficient business in Bradford for there to be built a piece hall which still exists as Piece Hall Yard in the middle of the city — surrounded, quite naturally, by several banks.

At the beginning of the nineteenth century men known as "wool staplers" collected the raw wool from large areas in and around Bradford and distributed it to the cottage workers. Such entrepreneurs grew rich very quickly and it was these riches that helped build roads, canals and other vital elements of Bradford's developing superstructure. One notable stapler was John Hustler who bought wool from 19 counties whilst his agents bought even more from another 14 counties.

Hustler had a huge warehouse where the wool was cleaned, sorted and classified. Thus staplers made vast capital fortunes whilst the individual clothier at the other end of the chain remained poor. Even in 1822 Hustler's estate was worth £12,000. And there were to be many more like him.

Prior to the above developments Bradford cloth had lagged behind that of other towns in the West Riding. It was inferior quality and produced only in short lengths (17 yards long by 1 yard wide was the size of an average 'piece'). However by the middle of the 17th century the length had grown to 30 yards and so Bradford started its climb up the wool trade league.

By 1810 Bradford was producing about 25% of all the worsted produced in the West Riding towns. The domestic system of weaving began to be dominated by the mills which were sprouting up all over the city. At one point 15 worsted mills were situated along the watercourse that ran through the city. Bradford's water supply was perfect for the task. Coming from the peat hills of the surrounding moors it was ideally soft for use by the dyers, bleachers and scourers. To the mill owners the same water was needed to supply their steam engines and being soft it did not "fur up" the boilers. So it was a very economic resource in that it reduced maintenance costs and required the use of less expensive soap.

❖❖❖

Readers could be forgiven for thinking, at this stage, that Bradford's success was built totally on local skills, the availability of wool (including wool from other regions) and good supplies of water. This is not so.

In fact the first mechanised mills in the city were powered by horses. What turned the pages of fortune for Bradford was the considerable supply of local cheap coal and the willingness of Bradford business people to use them to power their mills.

By the middle of the 19th century Bradford was the leader in the manufacturing of worsted, wool mix cloth and new fashion fabrics including silks and velvet. New fibres were introduced such as alpaca and mohair.

In 1851 Bradford was the base for 153 mills and the sky was dark with factory smoke. Meanwhile, about 10,000 hand loom weavers were living lives of the most abject poverty and social deprivation. Little of Bradford's new found wealth found its way down to their unfortunate level ....

The rich wool barons, however, did leave a wonderful inheritance to future generations of Bradfordians of gothic architecture, not all of which was demolished in the featureless pre-set concrete planning wave of the '60's.

❖❖❖

Towards the end of the 19th century Bradford became the focus of emigres from Ireland and Germany. The latter played a prominent role in the textile industries and have left behind a fascinating architectural legacy in that part of the city centre known as "Little Germany". By 1902 23 out of the 36 yarn merchants in Bradford came from Germany as did 31 out of 63 piece merchants. One merchant, Jacob Behrens had made a fortune of £40 million prior to his death in 1889. There is still a German church located near the city centre not far from the Bradford and Ilkley Community College.

The second World War resulted in emigres and refugees from many parts of Eastern Europe since incorporated into the Soviet Union and included Poles, Ukrainians, Lithuanians, Latvians and Estonians augmented by groups from Hungary and Yugoslavia. (In 1971 these groups accounted for most of the non-commonwealth population of about 4,500). As this book neared its completion nearly all these nations were beginning to strain against their Russian government and the struggle had begun to re-establish their own national identity.

The majority of migrants, however came from the Indian sub-continent, the first "pioneer group" arriving from Pakistan in 1940. Numbers rose from about 30 in 1944/45 to 350 in 1953.

Eight out of ten migrants who settled in Bradford by 1953 were night shift workers in the textile mills. Most of these were male.

In 1961 the census showed totals of Pakistanis (3,457), Indians (1,512) and West Indians (984). By 1966 the total of New Commonwealth immigrants in Bradford had risen to 13,410. The Asian groups came from a few localities in the Punjab and the Sylhet area of Bangladesh. About half were from the Mirpur district of Kashmir.

Hindus, Sikhs, Pakistanis and Bangladeshis all have different histories, languages or religions. Pakistanis and Bangladeshis have a common religion but not a common language. The rich mix of language to be heard in Bradford now includes Urdu, Gujarati, Punjabi and Bengali.

Bradford has thus become a fascinating patchwork of language, art, music, food and entertainment, much of it based on village cultures from other continents. Given that the indigenous culture stemmed largely from the existence of 17th/18th century English villages the concept of Bradford as one huge "village" is hardly surprising.

"Riches to Rags"

As seems to be the way with modern "progress", Bradford's wealth began to falter from the early 1950s due to mechanisation and external trading and manufacturing forces over which the city had little control.

Employment in textiles and associated industries peaked in the early '50's with 22% of the national textile industry's manpower being found in Bradford (55,734). The run-down then continued through the '50's, gathering momentum through the '60's so that by 1971 there were only 24,170 textile workers remaining in employment. Nationally, this decline in the textile industries represented a drop of 47% in employment terms. In Bradford the employment rate had dropped by 54% in the '70's. The impact was also felt by all those industries who supported the textile mills (e.g. light engineering).

In the mid-'70's Bradford's unemployment rate stood at 16% against the national average of 11%. 36,000 jobs just disappeared, never to return. It became the only area of West Yorkshire that then qualified for Assisted Area status in order that it could have access to much needed funding from central government.

The fourth largest metropolitan district in the country was practically on its knees. Morale was rock-bottom. Blacks and women were particularly loosing out in getting jobs as the scourge of unemployment spread onto peoples' lives. The air of decay was too obvious. People were losing faith in Bradford's ability to weather the storm. Major companies pulled out, adding to the misery. Investment from outside dribbled away to other parts of the country. Towards the end of the '70's and into the '80's it seemed like no-one wanted to know Bradford.

Part Two

Dark Days

Economic decline, with its awful social consequences of unemployment and poverty, was but one aspect of Bradford's misfortunes in the early '80s. Other dramatic events in the City were soon to intertwine themselves forever in the story of Bradford's worsening fortunes.

It is not easy to look back at such terrible happenings without once again stirring up, for many people, the same despairing feelings of loss and grief. It is difficult to describe such awful events — as if the City's image and reputation were the only important things to suffer as a consequence. However, the revolting and inhuman crimes against women by a mass murderer, the terrible loss of life in the flames at Valley Parade football ground, and the Ray Honeyford saga thrust Bradford onto the world's media stage. It is in that context that they are referred to here. If, as a result of the following brief references, the pain returns to those who still grieve, then the writer unreservedly apologises.

The Murderer Sutcliffe

In the middle to late '70's a man brutally slaughtered 13 women in and around his home town. The fear felt by the women of West Yorkshire of this criminal perhaps cannot be fully understood by those who lived outside the area at the time. It is unlikely that such fear could ever by fully understood by most men.

Special taxi-services were operated in order that women did not have to walk alone at night. Many women organised a complicated telephone system through which their movements could be monitored by friends, husbands, sons, etc. In this way their passage from point A to point B would be known and any delay in arrival would set alarm bells ringing.

In parts of Leeds, for example, women were escorted to, say, the end of their road and watched by their "protector" until they came into the view of either the person they were going to see or another "protector".

Bradford Council provided late night transport for its female staff who finished work during hours of darkness and had to get home.

Women, certainly in urban areas, were having to live their lives under a nightly siege of apprehension and fear that they might be the next victim of a mass murderer.

One of the brutal killer's final victims was a young woman student whom he savagely attacked and murdered as she returned from a visit to a pub near the Bradford and Ilkley Community College. Peter Sutcliffe was finally arrested for his appalling crimes against women in December 1979. Even before he had been found guilty at his subsequent trial, the fact that this monster was behind bars brought relief to many and in particular to the women in and around West Yorkshire.

At the time, and maybe for ever for some people, Bradford became synonymous with Sutcliffe and his foul deeds. The media duly carried out its duties and soon the whole world were making the connection between Bradford and the fact that it was the home of a mass murderer. Television screens constantly fed us pictures of Sutcliffe, his wife, his parents, his home in Heaton and even the graveyard where he worked. Bradford didn't seem a very safe place in which women could live.

The Honeyford Affair

Ray Honeyford was a Headteacher employed by the local education authority, Bradford Metropolitan District Council.

An article by Honeyford in a little known magazine set off a storm of protest which was to reverberate around Bradford district and the rest of the country for two years. The article was entitled *Education and Race — an alternative view* and it appeared in a magazine called the *Salisbury Review.* The article appeared in January 1984. The magazine had a specialist circulation of about 1,000 copies. Considering the minute number of copies produced, the article was to have a most profound effect on Bradford's race relations — which, up until the Honeyford article was published, had always been considered satisfactory although by no means perfect. That was an assumption that was now to be most dramatically tested and the result, many will say, was not a happy one for Bradford.

Ray Honeyford had joined Drummond Middle School in 1980 as its headteacher. The percentage of black pupils was due to rise from about 55% to 90% by the mid '80s. Within two years of being in Bradford he was disciplined by Bradford Council for a letter he had written in the *Telegraph & Argus.* His letter complained about a council grant that had been made to a local ethnic minority community association.

A major part of Honeyford's argument as published in the *Salisbury Review,* seemed to indicate his dissatisfaction with his employer's multi-cultural education policy. In normal circumstances the article may have been read by the magazine's 1,000 or so readers, mused upon and perhaps filed away on the bookshelf to gather dust. The rest of the world need not have known about the existence of the *Salisbury Review,* let alone the article itself. However, the fuse was lit and the explosion took place when the *Yorkshire Post* reprinted the article in the following March, 1985. The whole of Bradford, including the parents and children of Drummond Middle School, became aware of how their headmaster saw them — and, in their view, he didn't see them and aspects of their culture in too favourable a light.

A parents' action group was formed and Honeyford's sacking was demanded via a series of street demonstrations.

The Honeyford affair caught the national and international headlines and soon Bradford city centre was full of journalists and camera crews. Senior council officers with responsibilities for the Council's race relations policies were hounded by representatives from the media as they went about their duties.

For a short while an alternative school was set up by discontented parents. Towards the end of 1984 a series of negotiations took place between Honeyford, his Union and various officers of Bradford Council. The aim of these discussions was to arrive at a situation whereby Honeyford and his employer could part company on mutually agreeable terms. At one stage Honeyford was suspended for a few months and on his return was greeted by a picket line of parents and pupils and others who had a point of view on this, by now, emotionally complex affair.

You either agreed with Honeyford — or you didn't. There seemed little middle ground for anyone to take in Bradford. There were those who felt that the whole issue had been specially construed in order to alienate Bradford's ethnic communities. Another argument said that it was all to do with "free speech" and that Honeyford had a right to say whatever he liked. Until then, perhaps, it was felt that Bradford's race relations were an example to others. However, the many deep and emotive issues which arose from the Honeyford affair turned to expressions of anger from all sides of the argument. Such responses seemed to peel back a little of the veneer of a city that prided itself on its commitments to the ethnic minorities living within its boundaries. It is not an easy thing to do — for a city to re-examine its own heart and mind — while the whole world watches its every move and waits to see how it will get itself out of such a mess and still retain its dignity.

A terrible fire

Bradford City F.C. had become champions of the Third Division at the end of the 1985 season. Their home game against Lincoln on May 11th was to celebrate their ascent to the Second Division. It was just the kind of boost that many in the City felt would cheer people up. 11,000 people had crammed into the small football ground at Valley Parade, just off Manningham Lane and not far from the city centre to celebrate with "their team".

It is unlikely that the 2,000 people in the main stand were aware of certain letters sent to the football club from the West Yorkshire County Council which drew attention to certain safety risks at Valley Parade. One letter had read "The timber construction is a fire hazard and in particular there is a build-up of combustible materials in the voids beneath the seats. A carelessly discarded cigarette could give risk to a fire."

A meeting to discuss the contents of the above letter and to plan the demolition of the stand was arranged to take place on the Wednesday following the Lincoln game.

Yorkshire Television and Pennine Radio were at Valley Parade to record what should have been a much needed boost for Bradford. Something at long last to celebrate and perhaps help lift the social and economic gloom even if only momentarily. Instead, millions of T.V. viewers all over the world were able to sit in their armchairs and witness the most horrific scenes of death taking place as they happened.

A small fire had started at one end of the stand. The flames spread rapidly — "faster than a man could run". The roof of the stand was covered in tarpaulin and coated with asphalt which helped speed the journey of the awful fire. Some spectators died in their seats and included many children and elderly football fans. One father stayed in the inferno rather than leave his two young sons. An elderly man was led to safety by an 11 year old girl.

Fire engines sped from their city centre base only to find their way impeded by thousands of people fleeing away from the disaster. Water hose connections were broken as fire engines, ambulances and other rescue vehicles drove over them.

Most of the community around Valley Parade are of Asian origin. They opened the doors of their small terraced homes to take in the injured and the distressed. These kindly people, so often subjected to racist abuse by some mindless white people attending football matches, were doing what they could to help. Their actions on that day of Bradford's tragedy seemed, for a while, despite problems such as the Honeyford affair, to bring blacks and whites closer together.

The Valley Parade fire claimed 56 lives, most of them Bradfordians.

I was on holiday with my wife on the West Coast of Scotland on that dreadful day and returned to

Bradford a few days later. It is difficult for me to describe, looking back at that terrible occasion, what mood the City was in. What words exist that describe a community where nearly everyone you spoke to knew someone who had suffered either directly or indirectly? The City was undoubtedly in the most horrendous state of shock and bereavement.

Bradford Council moved quickly into action with Gordon Moore, its Chief Executive, playing the leading role. Gordon had been in the ill-fated stand with some civic guests from Germany and had left for the club house a few minutes before the fire had taken hold. The City Hall chauffeur was less fortunate, being a few seconds behind he was actually caught in the fire and sustained injuries.

By early evening Gordon Moore realized that the standing Emergency Plan was largely irrelevant for a disaster such as the one he had personally witnessed. What Gordon did was to mobilise council staff irrespective of their seniority or grade. Regardless of the Emergency Plan he gathered about him a group of people whose individual skills could meet the city's actual needs. This Disaster Team met the following Sunday morning. At 11.00 a.m. the first of many Press Conferences was held in City Hall before nearly 30 journalists.

Offices in City Hall had their usages changed within hours. Senior managers found themselves running errands to the photocopying room. Junior staff began helping to deal with the donations that started to flood in. The local newspaper (Telegraph & Argus) and radio (Pennine) joined the Council in launching an Appeal Fund which was to attract over £4 million from all around the world. The ground floor windows of City Hall were covered in hundreds of letters of condolences. Some letters were simply addressed to "Bradford". A special "Helpline" was also formed that Sunday morning as the Council's Social Workers gathered at hospitals to give assistance and support to the injured and to anxious or grieving relatives.

Within 24 hours of the disaster the people of Bradford had geared themselves up to cope with what was one of the most spiritually damaging events in the life of a city that, in other respects, was already on its knees. On the following Monday the high moorlands surrounding the grieving city were covered with a depressing thick, wet fog. "It seemed as if the very land was mourning the city it surrounded".

Many grim lessons were learnt as the result of the Bradford Fire and, in subsequent major disasters, Bradford's sad experiences became a benchmark against which the administration of resultant appeal trust funds would always be managed. A leading Bradford solicitor, Roger Suddards, gave much of his time and energy in both managing the Bradford Trust Fund and advising other communities who suffered similar tragedies (e.g. the sinking of the "Herald of Free Enterprise"). Similarly, the tragedy gave birth to a new approach to the counselling of the bereaved and injured in similar circumstances. Different skills were created by Bradford's social workers and these were soon in demand elsewhere in the country as, unfortunately, situations demanded.

For understandable reasons Bradford became the centre of world-wide sympathy. The rest of the country, and the world, watched as the community of Bradford struggled to come to terms with such loss. A day that had started in celebration had ended in disaster.

A memorial statue, donated by the people of Hamm in Germany, is located on the pavement opposite City Hall. It shows figures fleeing the flames and includes the names of all those who, so sadly, lost their lives.

Part Three

No Ordinary Council Report

In September 1984 Bradford Council published a report called *District Trends.* If the public were expecting a normal bureaucratic, statistically laden report then they were to be disappointed. Yes, the report did contain figures and information but their presentation was designed to provoke a new awareness of the social and economic problems facing Bradford and its people.

The report's foreword admitted that "it does not make pleasant reading". And many people in Bradford agreed. Some were even very angry that their City should have been portrayed in such a hard hitting manner. But honesty was a cornerstone of that document and the messages it contained had never been so clearly spelt out.

"DISTRICT TRENDS" warned of further economic decline, higher unemployment and the creation of "poverty zones" particularly in the inner city areas and council estates. It pointed out that there would be growing pressures on the environment and highlighted widespread inequality of opportunity, particularly amongst women and young blacks.

A major issue for Bradford, said *Trends,* was one fact unique to Bradford. Whilst many cities, particularly in the north, were suffering economic and urban problems, Bradford was uniquely faced with a rising population. This was particularly being felt in the inner city areas where land and resources were already under severe pressure.

(Latest forecasts (1989) show that by the end of 1991 Bradford will overtake Liverpool in population terms and so become the fourth largest Metropolitan District in the country.)

By 1984 unemployment had reached a staggering total of 37,000 which represented 18% of the working population. 50,000 people were on Supplementary Benefit. This was way above comparable national figures elsewhere.

The recession of the '70's and early '80's was now reaping its terrible reward. In the 20 years leading up to 1981 Bradford had in fact lost a quarter of its jobs. 45,000 jobs were lost in the textile industry alone. A new "unemployed class" was developing at a rapid pace in Bradford.

The District's race relations rightly came under the microscope in *District Trends.* Bradford, as indicated elsewhere in this book, is a city of many cultures. The 1981 census showed that out of the population of 464,000, about 1 in 7 (72,000) lived in households where the head of that household was born outside the U.K. Roughly speaking, this was broken down into the following distinct groups:

53,000 — India, East Africa, Bangladesh, Caribbean, the Far East and Pakistan.

6,000 — Ireland

13,000 — the rest of the world, including Eastern Europe.

Whilst it has often been assumed that Bradford's race relations could be described as "good" *District Trends* repeated that they were, in fact, practically non-existent. Social contact between communities was minimal and any formal contact was often restricted to the offices of the Community Relations Council. If problems did arise — and they did — the solutions were mainly devised by white people.

By 1996, the *Trends* report indicated:

that there would be the formation of a further 5,000 — 7,600 black families

that there would be a further 10,000 — 12,000 Asian children between the ages of 5 — 15 and

that a further 11,000 — 18,000 black people would be looking for work.

All this demonstrates just how unique Bradford is amongst other cities so far as its ethnic make up and population growth are concerned. Not surprisingly, as we will see later, the cultural riches of such a diverse people has made an important and positive impact on how Bradford lives as a community and how it is perceived by the outside world.

District Trends didn't just concentrate on racial inequality but also on the inequality that existed between the sexes in Bradford. The report asked "who governs Bradford?" and looked in depth at the District's poverty, housing, environment, health and welfare.

The report said (in its forword) — "... there is the unique nature of Bradford's problems. Along with the economic and urban problems faced by many cities, the District is also facing the largest increase in population of any Metropolitan District in the country and facing it in the inner areas where our resources and land are already under severe pressure ...

The changing face of Bradford will call for new ideas, new attitudes and ways of working and new relationships from all of us, members as well as officers."

District Trends carried with it the signatures of each of the major political leaders. They were in agreement that many things were going to have to change if Bradford was to survive as a socially and economically viable community. Their only differences were, perhaps, the methods whereby such crucial changes could be achieved.

The publication of *District Trends* by Bradford Council was, many declared, a brave thing to do. Certainly it acted as a mirror into which the City had to gaze whether it liked what it saw or not. In its reflection were images of a city which the majority of Bradfordians would find unacceptable. In effect this council report was saying "These are going to be our problems" — "What are we going to do about them?" It was the big question for Bradford.

Part Four

Bouncing Back

"We need to change our image"

City Hall, Bradford, is no boring concrete municipal office block. The Victorian fathers of the City had decided that an Italianate design would suit a building of such importance. Off to Florence went some intrepid architects and got out their sketch pads. The result of their efforts is reflected today in a building that is a replica of the Palazzio Vecchio, the Town Hall of Florence in Italy. Its clock tower reaches up into the Bradford skies like a huge extravagant monument to the woolmen who gave the city its early riches. Around most of its external facade are carved statues of the kings and queens of England. Their stone glazed eyes peer out over the passing traffic whilst they themselves remain frozen in honey coloured sandstone. Such romanticism does not detract from the fact that they also appear somewhat battered by Pennine wind, traffic pollution and the toiletry habits of starlings.

Inside the original part of the building there is an abundance of stone staircases, oak panelled rooms, glass domes and panes of stained glass leaded windows. Many of its corridors contain floors built with huge paving blocks of Yorkshire stone worn down in many places to smooth curves as a result of the millions of footsteps. The gloriously appointed circular council chamber, where the local politicians wrestled with the social and economic dilemmas of Bradford, is rich in polished mahogany. The floor slopes down to the centre as if reflecting the geophysical bowl like shape of the City outside its ornate walls.

It was in this unlikely monument to Italian architecture that I worked as a member of the Council's central Industrial Relations Unit. With a work force of about 26,000 employees and about a dozen separate unions life could be pretty hectic. The fact that the organisation seemed to be in a constant state of re-structuring did not help matters. People ran round stating "It's all about being able to manage change". Part of the difficulty was discovering how to change the way we were managing change, if you see what I mean .....

❖❖❖

One day, early in January 1986, I was summoned to Gordon Moore's office. As one of the Council's three Industrial Relations staff, day to day contact with the Chief Executive was negligible, so I was mildly curious as I made my way down spiral staircases, through the stone flagged corridors to his oak panelled office.

Gordon Moore had been a member of the national committee that was responsible for the massive national re-structuring of local government in 1974 (two years before I joined Bradford). Gordon was not "your average local government chief executive". He had a forthright, down to earth manner and would stand little nonsense from anyone — including elected members. Some liked him for this, others did not.

As I parked myself in his office Gordon began to relate a story to me in his very distinctive deep and somewhat booming voice.

"A group of people in the City are extremely concerned about Bradford's image" he began. "It has been suggested that unless we do something about the way Bradford is perceived, both internally and externally, the future will look very bleak indeed".

I recalled a conference held earlier at Bradford University to which about 200 senior representatives had been invited from every aspect of the City's life. (Police, Church, Colleges, University, Council, Chambers of Trade & Commerce, Voluntary Organisations and the top bosses from nearly every part of the private sector). The conference consisted of several workshops with the aim of trying to identify the way forward for Bradford in the 21st century. The conference slogan had been "Working together for a change".

Out of that conference came many recommendations, but nearly every group had identified the "big one" — Bradford's image.

Who was going to invest in a city that was finished and about whom cheap comedians got themselves a laugh?

Sat in the Chief Executive's office I listened as Gordon Moore continued. "Some of us have been to Glasgow to have a look at their *Smiles Better* campaign and to see what kind of impact it has had on the city, its people and its reputation." He paused.

I said something like "It all sounds very interesting". What else could I say? I was waiting to see, in the unfolding scenario, what the industrial relations implications were going to be for the Council and its workforce.

"We think Bradford should have a similar campaign, but obviously it would be unique to the District" said Gordon. "I've allocated £30,000 from my budget, the *Telegraph & Argus* have promised £10,000 and the Chamber of Commerce are to give £5,000."

"£45,000. That's a good start", I commented.

"Yes it is", Gordon responded "But it's going to need a lot more brass from somewhere else. Not only that,

we will also want someone to head the project up. To help plan and then direct it."

His eye caught mine just for a second. Have you ever had that feeling that something is going to happen to you from a completely unexpected angle, out of the blue, something you haven't been considering?

"Who do you have in mind?" I asked, almost knowing the answer already.

"Your name has been mentioned" said Gordon, studying my face carefully.

"But I know nothing about this kind of work." I said.

"Neither does anyone else much. It should be fun finding out", Gordon replied, smiling.

A little overwhelmed, I said, "I don't even know where to start."

Gordon said "Arrange to meet Terry Quinn and Donald Woodcock. They'll help us to get the ball rolling." He gave me the respective telephone numbers as I left.

I remember walking back to my office thinking "Who on earth are Terry Quinn and Donald Woodcock and what am I being dragged into?"

Little did I realize then that my career was about to take a huge and unorthodox lurch in another direction.

❖❖❖

Early in February, 1986, the three of us sat in a rather dingy committee room buried in the bowels of City Hall. We sat round a table that was ready for a jumble sale and on chairs that weren't much better. On the table, in effect, lay £45,000.

Terry Quinn was the Glaswegian editor of Bradford's paper the *Telegraph & Argus*, known by its readers as the *T & A.* Terry had been a member of one of the early "scouting" trips to his home city to look at the *Smiles better* campaign. He realized that in any campaign the involvement and support of the local newspaper was essential towards any chance of success. His editorial skills and knowledge of getting messages across to the public were to become a vital component in the months to come.

The third member of this seemingly unorthodox trio was Bradford born Donald Woodcock who was Chief Executive of Bradford's Chamber of Commerce, the largest, in membership terms, in the country outside London. He worked hard for his membership and his city and was at his desk often before I climbed out of my bed. Donald had seen the fluctuations of Bradford's economy for many years. His understanding of the different commercial sectors in Bradford and their relationships to each other was a most important ingredient in the task set before us.

The differences in our background, training and professional skills did, at first, seem quite unrelated to the project. This was a short lived assessment as, collectively, we realized the serious shortcomings of Bradford's image and the subsequent threat to its economic and social well being if that image was to remain unchallenged.

We had never worked previously as a team together although Donald and Terry clearly knew each other's sense of humour and this helped in those early days as we groped our way forward through endless "breakfast meetings". I certainly had never been in any direct contact with newspaper editors or Directors of Chambers of Commerce. However, such things rapidly became irrelevant. The significant issue for me was to realize that here were two people with important

and time consuming roles to play in their respective organisations and yet they were giving not only financial support but that other costly commodity — time. It was a generous gesture and was an early indicator that I was in the company of two people who were determined to make any campaign work.

We did two things immediately. We asked a leading Bradford firm of solicitors, Last, Suddards Ltd., to create a private company. We also issued a "challenge" to all Bradford based advertising agencies. The challenge included a brief resumé of Bradford's problems of image as we saw it and went on to describe how we wanted a campaign that would:

- alter the perceptions held by the outside world of Bradford and its people
- raise the levels of Bradfordians' self-esteem
- encourage inward investment into the District.

There was a varied response. Some, surprisingly, didn't even respond — maybe they thought the task impossible.

After a shortlisting process we invited about six agencies to pitch for the contract over a period of two days. The presentations were held in the *T & A* offices and we had invited Gordon Moore. Two leading councillors also attended, reflecting the "hung" nature of Bradford Council at the time.

It was, for me certainly, the first time I had to sit and watch advertising agencies go through their "pitch". One agency had taken as their theme "My kind of town" which relied on the Frank Sinatra hit song of the same name. Those gathered did not appear over impressed and this was observed by the agency's presenter who volunteered the information that he and his colleague had re-written the lyrics so that they focused on Bradford instead of Chicago.

At this point they produced a "flip chart" with the Bradford lyrics written on separate sheets. We still looked unimpressed.

"Shall I sing it?" asked the aspiring agency man.

"If you feel it would help," replied Gordon Moore, with what I detected was a bored expression on his face.

Now, I like the Birmingham accent. After all I do have a pronounced regional accent of my own. This chap launched into his song which was unaccompanied — but we all knew the tune, more or less. However our Brummy Sinatra had an ergonomic snag. The flip chart was behind him as he attempted to sing to us sat, expectantly, in front of him. Bravely he swivelled his head through 180 degrees as he sang. After a few verses it became apparent that "ole blue eyes" was singing too quickly for his colleague to turn the paper over for the next verse. The singer then tried, whilst singing at the same time, to instruct his colleague to turn the pages over more quickly. She, however, didn't appear to apprehend what his problem was and stood smiling at the small audience. As the whole "act" deteriorated, the Brummy accent increased and the unease of those observing this performance began to grow a little hysterical. Fortunately no one broke into outright laughter and Bradford's challenge to Frank Sinatra was soon forgotten.

We shortlisted three possibles and out of this we selected **Bradford's Bouncing Back!** as our slogan and a bouncing bear as the logo and mascot. The fact that a bear had nothing whatsoever to do with Bradford baffled some people. But as the civic badge of the City consists mainly of a **boar's** head we couldn't afford any obvious play on words ...

We were also registered as a private company, limited by guarantee and began trading under the name

Bradford Bounce Limited. The main aim of the company was reflected in its Memorandum of Association, clause 3(a) which read:

> **"To promote the industry, commerce, art, science and education of Bradford, to improve the image of Bradford both locally, nationally and internationally and to improve peoples' perceptions of Bradford, to inform such people of the qualities of Bradford and to pursue such campaigns as may be necessary for the purpose of fulfilling this object."**

Written like this it seemed a very tall order indeed. But at least everyone knew what we were about.

❖❖❖

The first major step, we thought, was to increase the number of directors of Bradford Bounce Ltd. We had already appointed Eddie Fenn who was then Bradford Council's Principal Marketing Manager as the fourth director. Eddie had worked hard to get Bradford onto the tourist map. The travel business had laughed at the thought of people flocking to Bradford — **as tourists!!** but he and his small team in the Council's Economic Development Unit had the last laugh as the District soared up the tourist league collecting several awards on the way.

Further new directors were recruited at a meeting in the Chamber of Commerce held in the summer of '86. The selection method was unique. Every aspiring candidate for the remaining four places put their names into a glass and a draw took place. Our lawyer, who thought this rather odd and only just legal, took note of the names as they came out of the glass. They were:

Judith Donovan a leading Bradford businesswoman with a successful group of companies to her credit.

Troubleshooting with Sir John Harvey-Jones, M.B.E.

John Piercy manager of the Bradford's Littlewoods Store Ltd.

Jean Hunter Head of Marketing and Publicity for the National Museum of Photography, Film and Television — one of Bradford's leading tourist destinations.

Dennis Walsh Director of a local travel agency and at that time president of the Chamber of Commerce.

We were now a board of eight, and, because I was sitting nearest to the lawyer, I was made Acting Chairman.

❖❖❖

Lots of things began to happen all at the same time. I was nominally still employed as an Industrial Relations Officer for Bradford Council. But as the *Bounce* project began to heave and grow around us my time sat arguing the toss with trade unions seemed to reduce almost daily and it was becoming clear that I couldn't go on doing two jobs at once.

❖❖❖

We began to work closely with the agency in producing a small feature film which we thought was essential for presentation purposes. The forecasted cost of such a project was going to take away a huge chunk of our initial £45,000 and I think some people thought this was not a wise thing to do at such an early stage of the game. We had viewed Glasgow's promotional video which, whilst attractive, consisted mainly of stills, captions and voice over. Because we had to consider television broadcasting in mind for our product we considered that a professionally produced mini "feature" film would be more appropriate.

To "star" in the film we engaged Billie Whitelaw, a Bradford born actress of international repute and Leslie

Sands, again a well known locally produced television actor who was fiercely proud of his Bradford roots.

Other Bradford born personalities who agreed to help their home town out were Harry Gration and John Helm, both well known local television presenters with the BBC and Yorkshire Television respectively. They both kindly agreed to appear in our film.

Neither Donald, Terry or myself had written a film script before and it was quite a learning exercise for the three of us. But the basic format was easy enough. The opening shots would be deliberately black and white and "grainy" showing dilapidated mills being demolished, unemployed kids on street corners and some of the terrible housing conditions in parts of the inner city. These pictures were produced against a stream of "anti-Bradford" jokes of the worst kind by a night club comedian.

The film then switches suddenly to bright and positive colour and highlights all that is positive about the City and its people. Leslie Sands takes us around the high tech developments going on in the area and points out that Bradford is the home of Grattan, the mail order giants, the International Wool Secretariat, the headquarters of the National & Provincial Building Society, the Yorkshire Building Society and the Bradford & Bingley Building Society.

Sands relates the excellent local industrial relations record that exists in Bradford and the success of companies like Spring Ram — did you know that one in every four domestic baths in the U.K. was produced in Bradford? Neither did I.

The film moves on to indicate the huge investment going on in the City which at that time (1986) was just over £½ **billion.** Hardly a City that was finished! Billie Whitelaw, against the dramatic backcloth of Ilkley

Moor, sings the praises of the countryside on the City's doorstep and tells the audience about the success of the Alhambra Theatre "recently refurbished to the tune of £4m including aid from Europe. And the amazing National Museum of Photography, Film and Television which was attracting millions of tourists. "Bradford? A cultural desert? Don't make me laugh!" ends Billie.

Towards the end of the ten minute film Leslie Sands' marvellous gritty face fills the screen as he firmly declares "… that's why we're fed up with the smears, fed up with the snide remarks, fed up with the way we're treated by the national media. **So what are we going to do about it?**"

At this point the screen is filled with a huge question mark. This **was** the question that Bradford had to ask itself and come up with a workable answer in response. Why should the people of Bradford be ashamed of their birthplace, be the butt of endless, often racist jokes and suffer economically because no-one wished to invest in them and their skills and thus feed the monster of unemployment?

The rest of the film provides the answer by describing how *Bradford's Bouncing Back!* was to operate. The film cost about £26,000 but, as will be seen, was worth every penny in public relations terms.

We called the film *Laugh? I nearly went to Bradford* which I remember thinking would make a good name for a book one day.

❖❖❖

In addition to the film we designed and ordered thousands of T-shirts, mugs, badges, car stickers and posters. We booked advertising hoardings in and around the city centre. A local toy manufacturer designed and produced hundreds of toy teddy bears complete with little badges declaring **Bradford's Bouncing Back!**

By about August/September time of 1986 we were in a position to plan two launches. The first one would be to the private sector whilst the second, depending on the success of the first would be to the public at large — all 430,000 of them.

In looking for a central figure around which a launch could be focused we went no further than Bradford's own University. Its Chancellor was Sir John Harvey-Jones, M.B.E. At that time he was still Chairman of I.C.I. and had, earlier in the year, been voted as the Guardian's *Businessman of the Year.* Sir John promised and gave his unstinting support to the project and was delighted to play the host on the evening in question.

Something else was planned for the launch, the ultimate significance of which no one could even guess. It was suggested that, because the campaign's logo was to be a bouncing bear we should have six appropriate costumes designed. The idea was that the bears would be present during the launch to complement the showing of the film. There were some hilarious scenes in City Hall when various bears were interviewed and physically examined.

"Is the fur fire-proof?"

"Oh! I don't know. Will I have.to stand near a fire?" came a muffled voice from inside a huge bears head with staring lifeless eyes.

"We don't know yet. But what about cigarettes, for instance?" I asked the animal standing in front of me.

The bear replied "I don't smoke."

"No!" I said "What happens if a cigarette accidentally comes into contact with your fur?"

After a while the whole interview dissolved into

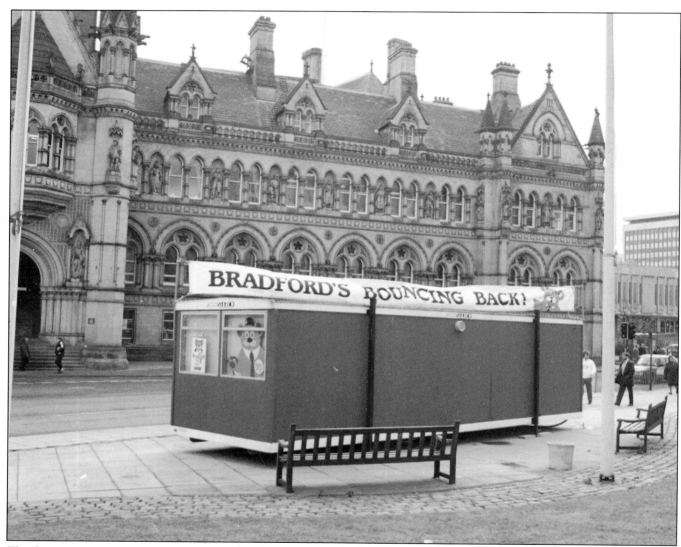

The Campaign's first home opposite Bradford's Italianate City Hall from November 1986 until March 1988

With former Prime Minister the Rt. Hon. Margaret Thatcher M.P. at Bradford City's football ground

farce and the bear removed its head remarking "Thank God for that, I'm sweating like a pig."

"Inside" the bear was a young ex-student by the name of Jane Whittaker. Like me, she was also born on the banks of the River Mersey. Jane had studied art and design at the Bradford and Ilkley Community College, which in an earlier time had produced one of Bradford's world famous artists, David Hockney.

❖❖❖

At the beginning of October, 1986, several hundred people were invited to a "special event concerning Bradford's future". Nearly every section of the City had been invited, the Lord Mayor, leading politicians. M.P.s, business people, major retailers, the police, the church, the educational establishments, trades unions and many, many others.

These were the people who had a stake in Bradford's future and whose individual interests were being directly or indirectly influenced by Bradford's image in the eyes of outside observers. Many of the business folk were long established family firms and had seen Bradford battered economically and socially as a result of unemployment. These and all the other guests would be asked to pledge money in order to finance the operation of the Campaign. Remember, we had already spent most of the original £45,000 "starter fund" from the Council, the Chamber of Commerce and the *Telegraph & Argus*. Failure to raise sufficient funds on this one night would have placed many of us in extremely embarrassing positions indeed. Certainly, if it didn't work, there would be no second chance.

On the night of the launch, 12th November, the splendidly decorated French Suite of the Midland Hotel was packed with huge round tables. It was dominated by a huge screen upon which the film was to be shown

to an unsuspecting audience. Behind the stage we had a digital display upon which we hoped we would be showing the rising sum of donations.

None of the audience had much of a clue as to what was going to happen. Their invitations had been deliberately vague saying that "if they were interested in Bradford's future Sir John Harvey-Jones had a message for them."

In just thirty minutes, egged on by Yorkshire Television's Richard Whiteley, the private sector representatives pledged £62,000. The team of six bears sweated their way from table to table and then to the stage to hand over completed pledge forms, a copy of which had been left on each seat.

The *Telegraph & Argus* filled the front page of the following day's edition with a massive headline that said quite simply ***Blast Off!***. Terry Quinn had ensured that the *T & A* was delivering the first big shot in Bradford's fight back. Supporting pictures showed some of the business people who had pledged financial support. From a one-man textile business to the boss of the Bradford-based Grattan mail order giants — the money had rolled in.

The fight to get Bradford up off its knees had begun.

❖❖❖

By now I was getting more and more involved in the campaign on a daily basis. My colleagues in City Hall saw little of me as Bradford Bounce Ltd began to plan for the public launch two weeks later. We arranged with Bradford Council to use the City's Christmas lights "switch on" ceremony as the way in which we would launch the campaign on Bradford's citizens. So, on a very rainy and dark November evening, on a leaking stage built onto City Hall's main steps, a young entertainer, Bonnie Langford, switched

Bradford's Christmas lights on. In front of a crowd of about 2,000 rain sodden Bradfordians a huge furry bear lumbered on to the stage to make its first public appearance. Little did anyone realize at that time, certainly not me, the extent to which this "animal" would figure in the months to come.

Tales from a Campaign

Early in January 1987 I was finally seconded to Bradford Bounce Ltd as the campaign's full-time Director. Little did I know, at the time that I would never return to the world of Industrial Relations.

❖❖❖

The huge transporter reversed on to the pavement opposite City Hall, bringing Bradford's city centre traffic to a halt. It was January 4th, 1987.

"Hell!" I thought "Perhaps I should have told the police."

The transporter's cargo was a huge portable hut, painted a scruffy green and was the kind of building you would see gracing building sites. The engineers from the Yorkshire Electricity Board and British Telecom were on site waiting to connect the hut to their services.

A chance comment by a local journalist had given me the idea that the campaign's H.Q. should be "on the street". We didn't have time to get a "real" office so this hut was going to be the focal point.

A few days after the hut was installed I was summonsed before the Council's planning boss.

"It's about this green portakabin," he began.

"What about it?" I asked.

The Chief Planning Officer's eyes narrowed.

"Look Tom. It's not exactly a monument to the City's architecture and is not very pretty to look at. Besides, it's sitting in the middle of a prime city centre site that we're trying to make attractive," he explained patiently "It's not exactly the kind of thing that we wish tourists to see. It's so ugly and scruffy looking. Can you do something about it?"

"Yes" I replied. The hint to move the hut was very strong indeed.

Two days later the hut stood resplendent on the same site, freshly painted in yellow, black and white. A banner stretched from one end to the other proclaiming *Bradford's Bouncing Back!* Whether the hut ever fitted into the planners scheme of things for the city centre is a debateable point. What few people had realized was that I had cajoled another council department to paint it with left over paint ....

But within days the siting of the hut paid off. An article in the *Sunday Telegraph* referred, in passing, to a "disused builders hut that seemed to be proclaiming that the city was bouncing back." I wrote to the paper explaining the purpose of the hut and what it represented. The piece appeared in the following Sundays' edition of the paper. The campaign had had its first taste of national publicity and I was learning to take every opportunity that presented itself to get Bradford's message across.

The hut performed its public operational role admirably as a distribution base for T-shirts, car stickers, badges, posters and toy bouncing bears etc., but it was not ideal as an administrative base. Help, however, was soon on its way from the National Provincial Building Society whose huge skyscraper headquarters jointly dominated the city centre horizon

Playtime with some of Bradford's mentally handicapped children

in company with its much older neighbour, City Hall. I was offered, on a no-charge basis, a corner of the Data Control office on the first floor of Provincial House which was about 100 yards from the "bounce" hut outside on the pavement.

Two things happened simultaneously in that first week of the campaign. I realized I needed help as the people of Bradford started to book the bears for a whole range of activities. The media also started knocking on the door to find out what the campaign was all about.

I rang Jane Whittaker.

"Hello Jane, it's me, Tom Clinton. Help!"

"What's up?"

"The bears. I'm getting requests for them to attend a Teddy Bears picnic, a new shop opening, a charity fun run and the Lord Mayor wants to know if the bear can help him plant a tree. Not only that the BBC want to film inside the hut next Friday."

Jane laughed.

"What do you want me to do?" she asked.

"I need to get people inside the bear costumes. What are you doing right now?"

"I'm still running this Community Arts Centre in Thornton" she replied.

"Well, how about becoming the campaign's Events Organiser?" I ventured.

There was a pause. "What exactly does that entail?" asked Jane.

"I've no idea" I replied "We'll have to make it up as we go along."

A week or so later Jane became the second employee of Bradford Bounce Ltd. She was occupying the hut and dealing with all the "off the street" enquiries as well as selling the campaign's merchandise. It was from here that Jane organised her bears. Bear "bookings" got so frantic that we had a huge board in the hut which showed where the bears had to be.

Jane used her powers of persuasion to coerce friends (mainly students from the Bradford & Ilkley Community College) to get inside the bear costume.

A short while later Jane and I were joined by David Walters who was invaluable in keeping the books and chasing sponsors for their promised cash.

One end of the 30ft long hut became the changing room for the bears. To say it was cramped in the hut is a massive understatement. There would be days when chaos ruled ...

"Jane!" yelled a muffled voice from the changing room.

"Yes! What do you want, Richard? I'm on the 'phone," Jane shouted back.

"Where's the pin for my crotch?" Richard (a new bear recruit) pleads.

The hut door opens. It's a BBC researcher wanting to talk to me about a potential piece about the campaign. I'm discussing T-shirt sizes with two American students over in Bradford on holiday. Another 'phone rings. Richard, comes out of the changing room, his costume complete except for the fact that his bear head is missing and a dangling piece of fur flaps, unpinned, between his furry legs.

Jane screams at Richard "Get your head on. Bears are **never** seen without their heads in public! This was a "Jane rule" to be broken only on pain of death.

"Shall I come back later?" asks the researcher of me.

"Have you got a safety pin?" I replied.

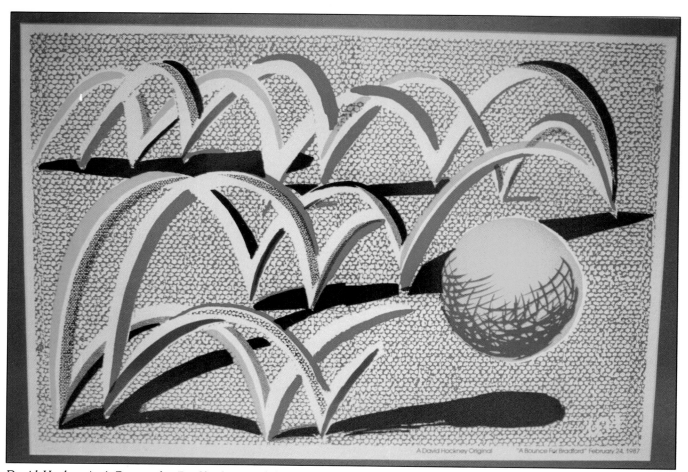

David Hockney's **A Bounce for Bradford** *- an exhibit at the Royal Academy's Summer Exhibition 1987*

A present for each of H.R.H. The Prince of Wales' children

One of the American students has a pin and kneels in front of Richard trying to pin the offending piece of fur back under his crotch. Such a job requires great skill and a steady hand. Richard, retreating under Jane's tirade, starts to walk backwards into his "den", dragging the American student along the floor with him.

I pick the telephone up.

"Bradford Bounce. Can I help you?" I shout above the din.

The noise in the background increases as a gang of schoolchildren burst in demanding free badges and car stickers.

"Jane. Can you deal with the kids please? I'm on the 'phone."

"No", says Jane, "Richard's got a pin stuck in his groin and we can't have bleeding bears. It wouldn't look right."

My telephone caller is impatient. So are the dozen or so kids. And the students. And the BBC researcher. And poor Richard, quietly bleeding to death in a headless bear costume ....

I pick up the telephone.

"Hello! Is that the ✱✱✱✱✱ campaign?"

"I beg your pardon!" I replied.

"I think the Council would be better off spending more money on filling up the ✱✱✱✱✱ holes in the roads rather than on ✱✱✱✱✱ bears. They're a ✱✱✱✱✱ waste of rate-payers money."

I began to explain that the campaign was run by a private company and we were not in a position to fill up any holes anywhere. The caller became hysterical and abusive and I had no option but to slap the 'phone

down, spilling a cup of hot coffee all over one of the schoolchildren. He screamed. Richard was screaming. The American students just sat there laughing.

The researcher said "Shall I come back this afternoon?"

"Please", I responded.

❖❖❖

Without doubt Bradford Bear was a major thread in the success of the campaign. Jane calculated that in the two year span of Bounce the bears had been invited to just over 600 separate events. This is remarkable for several reasons but the most surprising aspect was that we never advertised the public availability of the bears. The public demand grew and grew and the bears attended all kinds of events and functions. Pictures of the bear appeared in the press and on television in the company of such people as the Prime Minister, Leader of the Opposition, Natalia Makarova, the international ballet star, several members of Parliament of all political persuasions, David Hockney, H.R.H. The Prince of Wales, Everton F.C., London Festival Ballet, Bradford's Lord Mayor, Su Pollard, Adrian Moorhouse and many more personalities.

Through the simple device of making Bradford Bear available to the public and the media it was possible to place the ***Bradford's Bouncing Back!*** slogan in front of millions of people who, perhaps, had never even been to Bradford and, more than likely, held certain negative images in their heads. Because the bear was only associated with progressive and positive stories about Bradford and its people the success of the campaign began to feed off itself. But the ***Bouncing Back*** campaign was more than just a team of bears ....

❖❖❖

In February, 1987, Terry Quinn had the idea of asking

Security scare bear

David Hockney to make some kind of contribution towards his home town's campaign to change its image. This was done with the kind support of David's brother, Paul, ex-Lord Mayor of Bradford who, as a politician, had often brought a sense of well-meaning humour into Bradford's Council Chamber.

From his Los Angeles studio Hockney sent four sheets of card each representing a different colour to the *Telegraph & Argus.* The *T & A* then produced four matching printing plates which, when printed in sequence on the printing presses, resulted in a unique print. This print, which showed a ball making a series of colourful bounces, was titled *A Bounce for Bradford* and appeared as the centrefold in the *T & A* newspaper. Technically speaking, each copy was an original due to the manner in which it was compiled and yet when the process finished and the plates dismantled — there was no original left to see! The *T & A* sold its paper at its usual price then of 18p. In the letter accompanying his work to Terry Quinn at the *T & A* Hockney said "What happens when your presses put the plates together is the piece. It is, therefore, not a reproduction in the normal sense at all — the only way your image exists is on your page."

Thus the people of Bradford were able to buy Hockney prints for 18p a time from corner street vendors and newsagents on 24th February 1987. Shortly afterwards the print was selected to be hung at the Royal Academy's Summer Exhibition in London. In a previous exhibition Hockney had been criticised for the apparently excessively high prices he had charged for some of his works. The *T & A* printed another 10,000 copies of the *Bounce for Bradford* print which then went on sale at the Royal Academy at the original price of 18p. Purchasers were advised to treat the piece of art with magnesium methoxide in order to preserve it. It was the first tme that a piece of Hockney's had been produced using the above technique in a newspaper.

The publicity gained for Bradford and our campaign was enormous and certainly obtained international attention for Bradford. Not only that, we could also be sure that all over the world copies of the Bounce poster were being given pride of place in peoples' homes — and art collections.

But the Hockney connection doesn't stop here. The whole process described above has been captured by author Peter Webb in his biography *A Portrait of David Hockney* published by Chatto & Windus, 1988. The Bounce poster is reproduced in full colour in the book as an example of Hockney's artistic brilliance. It is, therefore, true to say that the campaign has "gone into the history books" and David Hockney is to be congratulated in helping to put his birthplace on the cultural map in such a unique and fascinating way.

❖❖❖

As the campaign progressed it soon became apparent that other "forces" were at work in giving Bradford a bad name. We discovered that all kinds of organisations were prone to stereotyping Bradford as a negative place as part of their business. Whether such stereotyping was deliberate or not we could never be sure, but Bradford appeared to be top of some subconscious list whenever something negative needed to be portayed to the rest of the country. Bradford Bounce decided to tackle such occasions as and when we became aware of them.

Take the matter of a national children's charity for instance. This very laudable and christian charity was seeking to raise much needed funds with which to ease the deprivation of "hundreds of thousands of children in Britain today". Part of their fund raising exercise included a national advertising poster campaign. The advertisement also appeared in the national press and many magazines as well as being displayed on huge bill boards all over Britain. The advertisement was centred around a picture of a young boy, aged two, called Peter. Peter had been photographed sitting on some awful scruffy stairs. He looked sad, dirty and underfed. Around his small feet lay heaps of garbage and litter. The caption to the picture made dismal reading about how many of the country's children suffer in a so called modern society. The advertisement also pointed out "that the photograph was not set up or reconstructed. We simply asked our photographer to record what he found in the cities of Britain".

The finished and published advertisement carrying the grim picture also carried the words "Bradford, 10 March, 1985" and the first sentence read "This picture was taken in Bradford". It was carried by many national newspapers and magazines and must have been seen by millions of readers. For example it appeared in the *Readers Digest* which has, I understand, over three million readers and the front page of the *Observer*. This was just the publicity that Bradford didn't want — we certainly were not asked to participate in such an advertisement! This was Bradford's problem — we were an easy target.

I rang the London based office of the charity in question and explained to their Director what we trying to do in Bradford. At first he couldn't understand what all the fuss was about but, to his credit, he later instructed his advertising agency to remove any reference to Bradford. Their campaign continued, only this time the photograph "was taken recently in England". On its own this might seem like a hysterical knee-jerk reaction and somewhat oversensitive. But why should a national advertising campaign specifically demean one particular place and then tell the whole world about it? The photograph may well have been taken in Bradford but there was nothing depicted in it that demonstrated particularly that it **was** Bradford. And why was it necessary to mention a specific town or city in such an advertisement? If such disheartening cases are nationwide then **that** is what should have been reflected in the caption and not just use Bradford as a bad and negative example.

During the above episode we discovered that one of the huge billboards carrying the "Bradford" advertisement was located directly opposite the entrance to H.M.S. Victory in Portsmouth. It must have been seen by hundreds of thousands of tourists and even in subliminal terms have created yet another negative layer of perception of a city perhaps most of them had never even visited.

❖❖❖

A well known national bus company produced its timetable covering its Victoria — Bradford/Leeds route. The small booklet contained a preface which sought to persuade bus travellers to visit Bradford where "from the top of surrounding hills one could look out over the rooftops of hundreds of Victorian slum dwellings". It transpired that the bus company's public relations company had used an extract from a very old town gazetteer. Strange publicity for a city trying to change its image and unfortunately, a city that has more than its fair share of housing problems. A live radio interview between the P.R. boss and myself soon elicited a public apology to the people of Bradford. Later, the bus company redeemed itself by featuring Bradford as an attractive place to visit in the first edition of its in-house magazine which was distributed

Bradford's Alhambra Theatre

A young bear fan

free to all its passengers (several hundred thousand per year).

❖❖❖

Even people in high places were "putting the boot in" on Bradford without realizing they were doing so. A high court judge told a student conference at Loughborough University that if they wanted to see where all the country's illegal immigrants were living "you should go up to Bradford". Unfortunately, for the judge, this was reported in the national press and soon got to us in the Bounce H.Q. I (and many others from Bradford including the then Lord Mayor, Mohammed Ajeeb) wrote scathing letters to the Lord Chancellor seeking a public withdrawal of such an unjustified statement.

No such apology appeared, though in a letter to me the Lord Chancellor (Lord Hailsham) did promise "to look seriously into the matter". A short time later the judge was "retired". It is up to the reader to guess whether or not the Bradford protest was instrumental in such a decision.

❖❖❖

Perhaps the most influential medium of our present age is television. Much of our knowledge of the rest of the world is flashed to us from the box in the corner of our sitting rooms.

A national television holiday programme decided to take a serious look at what Bradford had to offer prospective tourists. I sat down at home to watch the results. The opening clip to the Bradford piece was a panning shot over the roofs of streets of back to back houses. The camera cut to a fence of barbed wire with bits of plastic carrier bags ensnared and flapping forlornly in the breeze. The soundtrack accompanying the pictures was the theme music from *Coronation*

Street! I haven't watched this long running soap for years but last time I **did** watch it I remembered it was centred on Manchester. Clearly, the television people thought Bradford had been the subject of yet another boundary change. I rang the production office:

"This is the Bradford's Bouncing Back campaign — in Yorkshire!" I opened up.

"Oh good! What did you think of the programme?" asked the bright sparky voice.

"Most of it was excellent", I said "pity about the music though."

"What do you mean?"

"Coronation Street is set in Lancashire."

"Oh!"

"Why play music that had nothing to do with the subject matter?" I continued.

"We felt it was appropriate."

"Are you sure it was not a case of stereotying a grim northern image of back to back houses and barbed wire surroundings? After all it **was** about Bradford," I asked.

The debate went to and fro during the telephone conversation but in the end they conceded. They were seeking a northern stereotypical image in order to make the contrast with the rest of the piece — which was quite positive.

It could be argued that we should have been grateful to have had a TV programme at all. However, how many holiday programmes have you seen that go out of their way to show you the grotty side of a tourist resort? Not many, I bet. So why Bradford? Besides who knows how many people might have switched off as soon as they heard the music over such dismal pictures and not even seen the rest of the piece?

In July 1987 the *Spectator* published an article by a freelance journalist Richard West. In it he described his visit to Bradford and said

"Bradford is one of the most depressing and sordid inner cities in Britain" and that even a Third World city as poor as Bombay is more cheerful and safe. Our intrepid journalist then goes on to compare Bradford with Sodom and Gomorrah!

Sir John Harvey-Jones, who had launched the Bounce campaign, was quick to leap to the City's defence. His letter to the editor of the *Spectator* read:

"I have searched the article in vain for any mention of the efforts being made by all members of the community .... or acknowledgement of the very real achievements that have been made. I know many worse cities than Bradford .... and from my own experience, I feel far safer here than in Brixham. I don't know how, in his visit, Mr West managed to miss the National Photographic, Film and Television Museum, the Alhambra, the Colour Museum or take advantage of the tours in Brontë country.

There was no mention of the many achievements of Bradford University which was world standing in many of its activities and has one of the highest records of placing graduates into first time career jobs of any university in this country". (Just to remind you, Sir John **is** Chancellor of the University of Bradford).

His letter continued:

"The response of the whole community to the Bradford City Fire Disaster was an example of how this maligned community can and does pull together.

I am not a native or inhabitant of Bradford, merely someone who admires its multi-racial attempts to overcome horrendous inherited problems and deplores the kind of dismissive smearing that characterises Mr West's article."

I invited Richard West and the *Spectator's* editor to a further visit to Bradford. I wanted to treat them to the thrill of the huge IMAX screen in the National Museum of Photography, Film and Television, show them an award winning cemetery that had become a tourist hot spot, take them to one of the many international restaurants, walk them around Shipley Glen, visit the Brontë home in Haworth, do a show at the Alhambra, trek over the nearby moors ....

The *Spectator* declined the offer.

❖❖❖

In the very same month as the *Spectator* episode the *English Tourist Board's Annual Report* highlighted the success of the District's tourism. At that time, 1987, tourism was bringing in around £5 million to the City's starving economy. As the tourism drive was only launched in 1980 this represented a major achievement by Bradford Council's marketing team. Bradford had also become a destination on the Tourist Board's Great English City Breaks. The *Spectator* article missed this bit out as well ....

❖❖❖

By fighting back and protesting we were able to show everyone that the people of Bradford had had enough. The people of Bradford quickly realised that there was now a legitimate channel through which to register dissent whenever they felt that their City was being maligned. Each protest was given maximum publicity, certainly at local level, which then fed more stories into the media. Slowly, but surely, we were now winning the media war. That same media that was quick to carry "doom and gloom" stories about this incredible city was now aiding the bounce campaign to achieve its

National Museum of Photography, Film and Television, Bradford

aims by carrying more positive words and pictures. We were not denying that Bradford had immense social and economic problems. What we were saying was "Look at the good side as well" and look they most certainly did.

❖❖❖

In February 1988 the campaign's operational headquarters moved from its now familiar landmark opposite its Victorian neighbour, City Hall. The hut that had been home to Jane Whittaker and her bears was hoisted up onto a trailer, stopping Bradford's city centre traffic for the second time, and lurched out of Bradford with no ceremony whatsoever!

Our new home was peculiar to say the least. There will be many a Bradford man who will have purchased a new suit or shirt from O.S. Wain's shop on the corner of Broadway at the rear of City Hall. The leasehold of the property was held by Bradford Council and, on its expiry, *Ossie Wains* had its last once and for all sale and put up the shutters. Jane and I had paid an earlier visit and liked what we saw. The shop had been emptied of its stock but the interior remained exactly the same. There were small changing cubicles and mirrors all over the place and just heaps of room. Jane, who had been trapped in a 30ft x 6ft hut with no toilets for more than a year was particularly pleased.

After negotiating with the Council it was agreed that Bradford Bounce Ltd could move into *Ossies* on a temporary basis with the Bradford Festival organisation. Soon the campaign office became a rehearsal room for jugglers, acrobats, painters, musicians etc. The huge windows were soon filled with art, fashion and craft exhibitions produced in Bradford.

By early 1988 the *Bounce* slogan and logo was being seen all over the world. Visitors from Bradford to other countries were quick to take campaign material with them and then send photographs back to Bradford. A popular item of merchandise was the small toy reproduction of Bradford Bear and how that bear travelled! His first big trip was to the South Pole in the company of a local research scientist.

❖❖❖

A lonely servicewoman based on the Falkland Islands pleaded through the pages of the *Telegraph & Argus* for Bradford Bear to go out there and keep her warm.

❖❖❖

From Australia we received a photograph of the campaign slogan locally produced and strung across the length of a grandstand during an important national cricket match.

❖❖❖

We received reports from Peking that a convoy of tourist buses had to be distinguished from the local transport by the simple device of displaying *Bounce* car stickers on the front and back windows.

❖❖❖

A photograph appeared in the *T & A* showing a Bradfordian on the Great Wall of China with the slogan blazing out of his T-shirt.

❖❖❖

Canada, India, Pakistan, France, Germany, Hong Kong, North America were all recipients of Bradford's message.

Rumour has it that it was even seen in **Leeds!!**

❖❖❖

On one occasion I was invited to speak at a conference on *Place Marketing* in my home town of Liverpool.

*Sharing the **Telegraph & Argus** with the Rt. Hon. Neil Kinnock M.P.*

With the London Festival Ballet at the Coliseum, London

The conference room was sited in the prestigious multi million pound Albert Dock complex which was often the place to which my father would cycle as a docker. In those days, the late '40s to the end of the '50s, the dockside of Liverpool was a huge bustling maritime operation. My father would relate to me which ship he was unloading, where it came from, its cargo, its funnel colours and which shipping company owned it. As a child I often rode on the Overhead Railway (now demolished) which ran the length of the docks. From its elevated vantage point you could float over ships which were sailing to and from every continent. It was easy to see the growth and prosperity of this famous city, just as in Bradford at the turn of the century, the textile industry was creating a vital part of the City's history. Now, of course, the world had moved on and both cities were having to re-adjust, find new identities and attempt to re-vitalise their economic and social infrastructures.

I don't know what my father would have thought had he seen me in one of his docks addressing a conference and describing my role in trying to help Bradford to get back on its feet instead of Liverpool.

❖❖❖

In the Autumn of 1988 Bradford Bounce Ltd took stock of its position. The Board had reduced in numbers as a result of job changes for some of the directors leaving Donald Woodcock, Dennis Walsh and myself. A perusal of the accounts showed that, whilst we had a fair cash balance there was insufficient income being created.

As a private business, of course, we had to exercise our commercial responsibilities as directors and, after taking legal advice, it was agreed that Bradford Bounce Ltd should be placed in voluntary liquidation whilst there were some funds left in the bank. The effective date was to be 30th September 1988. Last minute negotiations with Bradford Council commenced in the hope that they would be able to take the campaign over. However, this was not to be.

Bradford Bear said his farewell to Bradford from the back of a lorry decorated by schoolchildren in the Lord Mayor's Parade as part of Bradford Festival on 23rd September, 1988. Waving a tear stained handkerchief, Bradford Bear cruised through the packed streets of the city centre and disappeared up Manchester Road.

The banner attached to the rear of the lorry read "That's all Folks!". The campaign had run for nearly two years.

On the 3rd October 1988 Bradford's Civic Society awarded its Annual Merit Award to the campaign for **"their dedication and success in promoting the overall image and the interests of the City of Bradford".**

Measuring the success

Nearly three years later the campaign is still being referred to in the local and national press whenever the regeneration of Bradford is mentioned. It still figures in school projects and a special video has been produced showing some aspects of its achievements.

But **what**, exactly, did the campaign achieve? The overall operating costs totalled £142,000. For this, Bradford had attracted nearly two million pounds worth of "free" media publicity. The local and national press attention alone equated to £1.2m had we had to purchase such publicity. Television and radio coverage made up the rest. All this publicity was, of course, showing Bradford in a positive and attractive light. Surely now, even those people who had never visited Bradford, would have their stereotyping images altered? In such an over-communicated world such as ours we were able to get our positive image across and that, too, had to be seen as a crucial success.

Locally, the level of merchandise sales clearly demonstrated that people were no longer ashamed of the word "Bradford". They wore it on thousands of sweatshirts, mugs, balloons, badges, car stickers, posters etc.

The small toy Bradford Bear was, of course, a great success with Bradford's younger generation and also (here I am sworn to secrecy) with some of Bradford's more prominent adults!! This was pride at street level. Letters to the *Telegraph & Argus* supporting the campaign far outnumbered the campaign's critics. Yes, there were those who thought the campaign was a waste of time and money.

Another degree of success was achieved in that several national institutions had been pulled up sharp when too ready to stereotype Bradford and its people. Maybe they would think twice now? One was now able to open up a newspaper and see positive stories about Bradford in addition to those that highlighted only the negative aspect.

We had learnt that it was possible to understand how the media worked, to work **with it,** and then influence it so that a more balanced view of Bradford was given to the public in general.

Other cities, too, were quick to spot Bradford's campaigning success and I travelled to such places as Liverpool, Sunderland, Leicester and Luton describing how we had organised ourselves. Queries and visits came from other cities including Belfast, Derby, Norwich, Wolverhampton to name but a few. Two consecutive editions of the *Derby Evening Telegraph*

in December 1988 carried double page spreads describing "the bouncing back of Bradford". All this good publicity for free! Who would have thought that Bradford, of all places, would become a reference point for the rest of the country on how to improve one's image!!" A few years earlier such a situation would have been seen as the same kind of joke as Bradford being a top tourist spot. At last Bradford appeared to be having the last laugh.

The Bounce campaign also demonstrated that, given a political focal point, it is possible for the public and private sector to work together for the overall good of the community. Obviously, local politics can never be ignored when mounting such a major public relations activity. This is particularly so in communities, like Bradford, where economic and social decline have been interwoven to create a seemingly continuous downward spiral of despair.

Bradford, of course, will always have its own unique and exciting political style, irrespective of who runs City Hall. A point worthy of note was that the campaign was launched whilst the Council was "hung", ran through a Labour administration, a further "hung" period and then a Tory Council for its final few campaigning weeks (September/October 1988). At no stage throughout this political merry-go-round was the campaign seriously detracted from its day-to-day aims by political interference.

To what extent the campaign played a role in the City's resurgence from the late 1980s onward can never be scientifically measured. But then, how is it possible to measure levels of pride and self-esteem amongst a community who felt, less than five years previously, that they and their City were doomed to economic obscurity?

If anybody asks me, and many still do, what made the campaign such a success, I am always reminded of part of Sir John Harvey-Jones' speech, in November 1986, when he launched the campaign. Sir John, said to those gathered:

"You have suffered in macrocosm what the rest of the country has suffered in microcosm. But you are a plucky lot. You are not prepared to lie down and accept defeat. You are generous and kind and will always fight back".

How right he was, because the success of the campaign, like the success of Bradford's future, was, and will be, due to the people who are proud to call themselves "Bradfordians".

Part Five

Turning the Corner

In November 1987 the Department of Geography at Glasgow University published the results of a nationwide survey of something called *The Quality of Life*. Thirty eight major cities across England, Scotland and Wales were ranked against a list of twenty variables. The survey showed that the most important aspects of the quality of life were considered to be:

- Low rates of violent crime
- Low rates of non-violent crime
- Good health service
- Low pollution levels
- Low cost of living
- Racial harmony
- Good shopping facilities
- Cost of private houses
- Access to areas of scenic quality

Other variables included employment prospects, wage levels, travel to work time etc.

Bradford came 6th in this national league and 2nd in England. London came 34th, Birmingham was last in 38th position.

Leeds was 27th.

In relation to Bradford, the report concluded that "...Bradford emerges as the top city for access to areas of high scenic quality. It also provides good shopping facilities and has low-costs of living and owner occupied housing".

It can be imagined how well such a survey was received in the City and across the country as a whole.

But maybe the report was indicative that things were changing for the people of the District of Bradford.

Discussions began to take place between major developers, the Council and other parties interested in making sure that Bradford bounced back. Soon the media was indicating that great things were planned for Bradford.

Towards the end of 1989 estimates showed that more than a billion pounds worth of investment was being planned for the City. These were no ordinary developments either ....

Take **Lister's Mill**. The Victoria & Albert Museum in London have chosen Bradford as the base for their regional "extension". An earlier feasibility study had already indicated that Lister's Mill in Manningham could provide a home for the location of some of the *V & A's* priceless Indian collections — most of it never having been seen by the public. One cannot ignore the connection between the period in which the London museum commenced, its original patronage and the era in which Lister's Mill was built.

Given that the Mill site is situated in the heart of a large Asian community the whole idea seems historically complete.

In addition the 12 acre site will become a village in its own right with shops, a hotel, offices, flats, workshops and an Asian Study Centre. The project is expected to cost more than £50 million.

The **Alhambra Theatre** had already been established as a prime theatre following a massive and imaginative restoration with the aid of cash from Brussels. Rudolph Nureyev, the great ballet dancer, described the theatre as "having the best dance stage in the world". The theatre now attracts theatregoers from all over the north and many a coachload is transported up the M1 .... from London!

Similarly the **National Museum of Photography, Film and Television** attracts millions of visitors from all over the world. As the home of the huge five storey high IMAX cinema screen the Museum must rank as one of the major tourist attractions in the north of England. This was recognised in 1989 when it was given the Museum of the Year Award. The media were quick to realize that Bradford had the potential to become a major communications centre in the North and the Museum now houses the Yorkshire studio of TV-AM, the national breakfast time television channel. Equally exciting is the plan for the country's first Cinerama Museum to be based there as an annexe to the main museum building.

If you drive into Bradford from the east you will see signs indicating the existence of a place called **Little Germany**. Once a run down area of deserted textile warehouses just off the city centre, the area has undergone an explosion of creativity. With Bradford Council's Economic Development Unit spearheading its revival, the once shabby streets and buildings are once again echoing to the sights and sounds of thriving commerce and businesses.

Bradford Council had worked very hard in obtaining massive grants from Europe and it is to their credit that Bradford's infrastructure has undergone major improvements. For example, new roads now circle the city centre taking out the heavy traffic that plague other comparable cities. European assistance on such a large scale is now directed elsewhere on the continent. Luckily, certain people in Bradford Council planned well in advance and obtained the benefits accordingly before the tap was switched off.

The private sector began to look anew at Bradford. Office rents started to increase. The best of the developable land was quickly gobbled up as the City's potential for the 1990s became evident. One of Bradford's major problems is the lack of good, flat and well located developable land. Thus pressure on Green Belt land for housing and industrial sites was another indication of the belief in the Distict by those with money to invest and from which jobs would be created.

Banks began scrubbing away at the front of their city centre offices and revealing more of that honey-coloured stone architecture so loved by the City's Victorian forefathers. Newly built offices sprang up, most of them being occupied by financial services, which further consolidated Bradford's position as a major financial centre.

Bradford has two central main line stations which, perhaps as a matter of constant regret, are unconnected despite the very short distance that separates them. One of them, **Forster Square**, is now the focal point for a massive shopping redevelopment to be known as Broadstones and covering 390,000 sq. ft. The company behind the project is Burton Property Trust who are investing over £50m into the prestigious project which, according to the *Telegraph & Argus* "will change the way thousands of Bradfordians will go shopping in the future".

A £46m scheme is planned to develop the end of the M606 motorway link into a **Silicon Dale**. This will be known as *Eurocam* and is the brainchild of Dr. Tony Martinez who had already brought high tech success to Bradford through his previous company, *Microvitec*.

Down the road in Shipley a huge Victorian Mill complex lies sprawling around the little village of

Saltaire. **Salts** is a six-storey textile mill which is being brought back to life under the guidance of a young entrepreneur, Jonathan Silver.

Built in 1853 part of the mill already houses a large collection of David Hockney prints in a most attractive gallery. (Hockney was born in Bradford and studied art at the local Art College). There is a £25m scheme planned to develop part of the complex into a Victorian "mill mall" and, already, several prestigious theatrical companies have taken full advantage of the huge weaving sheds to put on top productions (including a version of *West Side Story* in which the audience became a moving part of the action). Salts has attracted many hi-tech companies into its massive floor area.

But perhaps the one single project that is the *crème de la crème* in Bradford's changing fortune is to be the **West End**. This project, costed at over £250m is set to stagger the imagination. As probably the last major development of such a size for some considerable time in Bradford, it will also put the final touch to one of the most exciting periods of the City's history.

A company called 3-D Developments, based in Leeds, have put together the most ambitious and exciting ideas together in a comprehensive attempt to build a city centre actually designed by the community. Centering on the Alhambra and the National Museum of Photography, Film and Television the concept almost defies description. The office space created will total 500,000 sq. ft. as well as 100,000 sq. ft. of high street retailing.

It is intended that this development will include:

- the only electronic zoo in the country
- an Omnimax Theatre
- three pavilions representing the cultures of the East, Europe and of course — Yorkshire
- an exhibition and conference centre
- a 240 room hotel
- an Arts Centre
- a Health and Fitness Centre

The whole will take five years to build. It will be a fitting monument to all that has happened to Bradford in the last decade or so. The *West End* was designed as a result of workshops and consultations with as many groups of the community as possible. People were asked to give their views on what their city centre should look like and which minority groups should be especially catered for.

Parking — a major problem for Bradford — would also be helped by the inclusion of spaces for over 2,000 cars.

It is estimated that the whole scheme will provide the District of Bradford with around 10,000 much needed jobs.

The completion of the *West End* scheme is estimated to be somewhere in the mid-'90s and the day it opens will be the day that Bradford will be seen as a community ready to take on the 21st century.

Part Six

The Community Celebrates Itself

If ever you visit Bradford around about September time the chances are you will witness some strange goings on all over the District. Don't be surprised if you bump into a chap with fire spurting from his mouth or two young women dressed in startling coloured clothing swinging from a high wire in the middle of the city centre. And are you really watching hundreds of jugglers — yes hundreds — hurling thousands of items into the Bradford skies at the same time? And, yes, that is the sound of bagpipes you can hear as you pop out of the office for a lunchtime sandwich.

The idea that Bradford should have its own Festival was born in the mid '80s when Bradford Council wished to celebrate the opening of the revitalised Little Germany area of the city centre. It was decided to have some street entertainment which included music, performers of all kinds, dancers and jugglers. The person who played a leading role in organising this "one-off" event was a young man named Allan Brack who gathered round him a young enthusiastic team who set to work putting the festival together.

The Little Germany Festival was a great success and the Council were taken with the idea that perhaps a bigger and better event could be organised for the benefit of the whole community. Perhaps an annual festival?

Allan Brack and his team were set to work by Bradford Council and were soon calling upon a whole range of artists and performers that already existed in and around Bradford. With a budget consisting of a cash grant and other "help in kind" from Bradford Council, and some sponsorship from the private sector the festival team soon got together a workable programme which took place in September 1986.

The early days of the Festival took Bradford by surprise. So much so that street entertainers commented that the passing Bradfordians seemed "somehow afraid to stop and look". Had things gone so bad in Bradford that people were forgetting how to enjoy themselves? Maybe. People would often reply to the question "What do you think of the Festival then?" with "What Festival?" or "I didn't know there was one".

On one occasion, when the Festival organisers shared *Ossie* Wains empty shop with *Bradford Bounce* a magician stood in the window facing onto the busy street. He produced some really fascinating stunts of illusion to the passing shoppers — and that's what they did — went on passing. Clearly it was one thing to organise a lot of activities but another to get your audience to stop and watch. In those early days it almost seemed as if it was someone else's Festival and not Bradford's.

Allan Brack, joined by Dusty Rhodes and Jeremy Higginson and a whole team of dedicated creative people, were not deterred by initial obstacles and pressed ahead cajoling, persuading and enticing a vast range of people to make the Festival their own. A full time administrator was appointed as was a fund raiser in order to create a solid financial base from which to operate.

The Festival's basic strategy soon became clear and that was to make sure that all sections of the community took direct ownership of the two week event. It was not so much a case of saying "Look, here is a Festival that **we** have organised for **you,** please enjoy it." What the Festival organisers were saying to the community was "This is **your** Festival, produced by you, enjoy yourselves".

To put the above activities into perspective, it has to be remembered that they were taking place against some of the social and economic disasters referred to in previous chapters, a major scurge being that of unemployment. Whilst the *Bounce* campaign was focussed on reversing Bradford's negative image and poor self-esteem the Festival was encouraging the community to recognise that its very existence was worthy of celebration. The fact that you were of, say, commonwealth or eastern european descent and proud of your culture, was a vital thread in that tapestry we describe as "the community". The Bradford Festival Team — now a private company — were able to tap into this part of Bradford's phsyche and produce the most staggering results.

❖❖❖

Bradford Festival has, in effect, created a unique resource for the community — the opportunity to celebrate itself. What the Bradford Festival has achieved for Bradford is something you cannot read about in books (except this one!) or learn about in college. The historical and social make up of Bradford provides a ready made paint pot from which the Bradford Festival team have been able to paint, with professional creativity, the most incredible pictures of a multi-cultural community.

In 1990 the launch of Bradford Festival was centered around a huge 20ft. high silver *Trojan* horse which was hauled into the city centre by hand. From the belly of this equine monster dropped some steps down which a parade of breathtaking costumed figures proceeded to the sound of pulsating Asian music. The impact of this single inaugural scene was massive and it was an image soon repeated on the pages of several national newspapers. Space does not permit the description of the hundreds of different Festival events that now pull people to Bradford from all over the country and the rest of Europe. In any case, no two years are alike. There is a natural capacity for celebration within the people of Bradford which, somehow, the Festival team have skilfully identified and presented back to the community beautifully wrapped in exciting colours. The impact on the City's image and economy is not overlooked by Bradford Metropolitan Council as it continues to give regular financial aid, and assistance "in kind", to the Festival.

The local and national media are increasingly paying more and more attention to this unique community event so much so that its reputation now attracts other cities who wish to know "how they do it in Bradford".

But if there was one aspect of the Bradford Festival that gives it that "certain something" it is the way in which each community makes it own unique cultural contribution. The Bradford Festival team have developed a "sixth" sense when it comes to getting the different sections of the community involved in making the Festival what it is. In this respect, of course, Bradford is spoilt for choice. We need to remind ourselves that the district of Bradford contains well established communities from the Ukraine, Poland, Hungary, Latvia, Yugoslavia, Ireland, the Caribbean, China, Italy and Asia. Bradford Festival provides the stage — literally — upon which these communities can proudly demonstrate their pride in their own unique culture. In any one single day a visitor to Bradford Festival can experience several exciting international events — without leaving the District's boundaries! It must be one of the cheapest and quickest ways of seeing the world ....

A major Festival attraction that staggers even its organisers is the Asian *Mela*. In 1990 this open air event attracted about 100,000 visitors. The *Mela* (which roughly translated means a fair or bazaar) takes place over three days in a major outdoor venue (in 1990 this was Lister Park) and is a massive collection of stalls selling ethnic art, crafts, clothes and exotic jewellery. In addition, from all over the country, people come to experience the delights of a mouth watering range of international dishes. Added to this is the rich hypnotic mix of Asian music in all its different interpretations performed by groups large and small. Sometimes the music fuses west with east and the results can be at once both exciting, dramatic and emotionally draining. From time to time this music is accompanied on stage by exotically costumed dancers whose subtle movements can belie the drama and romance found in their dancing. People from seemingly different cultural backgrounds stand together before the stage transfixed by the rhythms. Some, almost unconsciously, start to sway and dance, inventing their own steps in time to the music. Do they, I wonder, realize that they are moving to music that probably originated centuries ago in a small mountain village in another land — another country thousands of miles away from this urban field in the middle of Bradford.

The full international flavour of Bradford Festival should not be under-estimated as is indicated by some of the names that cropped up all over the busy 1990 programme : Jaleo (flamenco music from Spain), Kozatski Zabavy (Ukrainian cossack dancing), Mamata Shankar Ballet Troupe (Indian dance), Krisnaleela (Indian shadow puppetry), Nachda Punjab (music and dance group), the Calcutta Drum Orchestra, Roberto Pla and Conjunto Fuego (Latin American Jazz), Moravia Serbian Dancers (Yugoslavian folk dancing), King Masco (Sierra Leone calypso), Shikisha (Zulu dance), Tazim Khan (Qawwalis band), Quimantu (Chilean music), and the Adzido Pan African Dance Ensemble (Kenya and Tanzania dancers and drummers).

❖❖❖

Out of all the above images (and only a fraction of the Festival has been described here) there is one that the writer of this book eagerly anticipates each Festival year. The Wool Exchange is a wonderful evocative Victorian building that reflects the City's history of wool and its impact on Bradford's economic standing in the 19th century. Bradford Festival have their offices located inside the building. During the Festival the inside of the building is transformed into a venue for a wide range of events. A stage is very cleverly constructed at one end of the wooden floor between marble pillars around which the ghosts of 19th century wool merchants no doubt still haggle and bargain, making and losing fortunes.

The back of the stage is overlooked by a huge white statue of Richard Cobden. The statue was sculptured by Mr. G. Booth, an American, as a donation to Bradford's Wool Exchange in 1876. Mr. Cobden's pale and unsmiling face looks out from the stage towards the Festival audience, a hand outstretched. Beneath him, with their backs to him and under a sweltering battery of multi-coloured lights, artists and performers go through their acts to the delight of their audiences. In one shady corner is a small bar and to the rear are some food stalls selling anything from samosas to pizzas and vegetarian salads.

I often wonder what Mr. Cobden would think of the Wool Exchange reverberating to a Bhangra band, or the sound of Bradford schoolchildren singing extracts from *Cats,* or the thump of a clown falling over yet again. Maybe Mr. Cobden was fond of a laugh himself? Did he ever think that the place where merchants once stood buying and selling wool all those years ago would now be full of entertainers? How would he feel about the ceiling of the Wool Exchange being bathed in brightly coloured streams of cloth like some huge Arabian tent with trapeze artists flying like birds through the air? And all these people dancing up and down on the wooden floorboards, surely there must be a rule about it? We'll never know any of this from the silent Mr. Cobden as he stands on his plinth, his stone glazed eyes staring thirstily at the bar.

The image I have is that, one day, during an interval in an Irish ceilidh, Mr. Cobden will suddenly yawn and stretch his 125 years stiffened limbs. Rather stiffly,

he descends from his plinth at the back of the stage and approaches the microphone. A hush falls on the amazed audience. Is this just another crazy Festival stunt? He gently brushes some of the years old dust from his pale grey Victorian jacket and, shading his eyes from the bright light with a trembling hand, he peers out into the audience as if seeking some old familiar faces in the crowd.

A deathly silence has fallen onto the dance floor. The accordian player takes a nervous sip of his pint of stout as this strange old man totters towards the front of the stage where he comes to a faltering halt. Is he about to rebuke those gathered for abusing his Wool Exchange with all this noisy dancing and singing?

In a persuasive voice that is soft, though somewhat hoarse, Mr. Cobden speaks to the paralyzed audience.

"Isn't anyone going to buy **me** a drink?" he pleads.

Festival at the Wool Exchange — Mr Cobden looks on

Epilogue

A journalist once told me that "There is something about Bradford that will always ensure its prominence in the national news. It must be something in the water or the stonework". Even as preparations for the publication of this book drew to a close, this remark came to mind as Bradford, time and time again, found itself under the national, and sometimes international, media spotlight.

From October 1988 until May 1990 the nation's television screens, radio and press showed the emotional reverberations of Bradford's Council Chamber. The Conservative Group held 45 seats, the Labour Group 43 and the Liberal Democrats two. These mathematics of democracy resulted in the Lord Mayor being given a second and decisive 91st vote. Many objected, and the people of Bradford District watched each time he raised his hand in the air when it came to the vote. By May 1991 the balance of power had changed and gave the Labour Group 53 seats, the Conservative Group 35 and the Liberal Democrats two.

City Hall, Bradford, again formed the backcloth against which millions of television viewers all over the world saw a copy of *The Satanic Verses* being publicly burnt by angry Muslims. This was part of the world wide furore caused by the publication of Salman Rushdie's book which had offended the Muslim faith.

A BBC2 television programme, transmitted on 22nd May 1991, included several repeats of the "burning book" scene on the national network.

Earlier, in May 1991, a six year old child, Rucksana Khan, was savagely mauled by a pit bull terrier. She was lucky to remain alive but suffered the most appalling injuries. This one incident, following others elsewhere in the country, was seen as the straw that broke the camel's back and the British government acted swiftly to introduce national legislation, itself the subject of further emotional debate across the country. Here was Bradford, yet again, featuring in the nation's news headlines.

As May 1991 drew to a close I rushed to get the manuscript of this book into an envelope so that I could post it to the printers. Apparently writers have deadlines to meet. Suddenly in the midst of my task, a television newsflash told me about the assassination of former Indian Prime Minister Rajiv Gandhi. The newsreader stared at me from the box in the corner, almost as if challenging me, and said "…. and for a reaction to this from members of the Hindu community in Britain we now go live to Bradford".

I thought of what the journalist had said and hurriedly sealed the envelope.

.... and another view

A specially created portfolio of photographs showing different aspects of a surprising place called Bradford.

Bradford, as perceived elsewhere — an old and dirty northern industrial city in decline.
Picture: David Blocking/Bradford Heritage Recording Unit

View across the City Centre earlier this century
The chimneys are not smoking because of a general strike.

Picture courtesy Bradford Heritage Recording Unit

View looking south-west across the City Centre from Undercliffe Cemetery.

Picture by Tim Smith/Bradford Heritage Recording Unit.

Traders stand on the floor of the Wool Exchange beneath the statue of Richard Cobden, 1904.

Picture courtesy of Bradford Heritage Recording Unit.

The wealth created during the City's reign as worsted capital of the world enabled the building of many fine Victorian buildings. Sadly many have disappeared, but some, such as Bradford Technical College, remain.

Picture by Tim Smith/ Bradford Heritage Recording Unit

Homes and factories existed side by side in the centre of the City

Picture by Christopher Pratt

Grattan's Mail Order boasts the largest fully automated warehouse in Europe.   *Picture by Tim Smith*

Sheep farming on the moors above Stanbury. Over half of the Bradford Metropolitan District is open space.
Picture by Tony Holmes/Bradford Heritage Recording Unit

New uses now have to be found for the old buildings of the City, such as Salt's Mill at Saltaire. As well as housing the Hockney Gallery it is also home to the northern base of the Commonwealth Institute, a multi-cultural educational resource centre. Here a local dancer, Josie Singh, performs at its launch in 1991.

Bradford is well known as home to its Asian communities. However it also has significant communities with origins in other parts of the world, for example Eastern Europe. The Ukrainian Orthodox Church is one of many places that cater to their needs.

Picture by Tim Smith/ Heritage Recording Unit

Each year the Mela, or Asian fair, attracts tens of thousands of people to Lister Park as part of Bradford Festival.
Picture by Tim Smith

The Annual Bradford Festival always succeeds in giving the City a positive profile in the local and national media. This extravagent festival launch introduced a varied three week programme in September, 1990.
Picture by Tim Smith